Level 2
Mid-Beginner

Shrek 2™

Popcorn ELT Readers

Meet ... everyone from SHREK 2™

This is Shrek. He is an ogre.

Shrek

This is Princess Fiona. She is an ogre too. She lives with her new husband, Shrek.

Princess Fiona

This is Donkey. Donkey is Shrek's very good friend.

This is Puss In Boots. He is a cat, but he can talk!

Puss In Boots

Donkey

This is the Fairy Godmother. She is good at magic, but she is not kind.

This is the King and Queen of Far Far Away. They are Fiona's mum and dad.

This is Prince Charming. The Fairy Godmother is his mum.

These are the fairy tale characters.

Before you read ...
Do you know these fairy tale characters?

New Words

What do these new words mean? Ask your teacher or use your dictionary.

frog

This **frog** is yellow.

bottle

This is a **bottle**.

handsome

He is a **handsome** man.

castle

This is a **castle**.

husband

She loves her **husband**.

kill

Cats **kill** small animals.

kiss

magic / magician

This is a **magician**.
He does **magic**.

ogre

This is an **ogre**.

party

They are having a **party**.

'Once upon a time ...'

The book starts **'Once upon a time ...'**

Verbs

Present	Past
drink	drank
find	found
think	thought

SHREK 2™

CHAPTER 1
Once upon a time ...

Once upon a time, there was a beautiful princess. Her name was Princess Fiona. The King and Queen of Far Far Away loved her very much.

But at night Princess Fiona was an ogre!

The King was frightened. 'What can we do?' he asked the Fairy Godmother.

'I'm going to take her to a dark castle!' said the Fairy Godmother. 'She can wait there for Prince Charming. One kiss from Prince Charming – and Fiona's a princess and not an ogre!'

Princess Fiona went to the dark castle. The King was very sad.

After many years, Prince Charming came to the dark castle. But he did not find Princess Fiona, he found … a wolf!

'She's not here,' said the wolf. 'She's with her new husband.'

'Her husband!' shouted Prince Charming. 'Oh no! I'm late!'

CHAPTER 2
'Come to Far Far Away!'

Princess Fiona's new husband was Shrek. He was an ogre too. They lived in a small house and they were very happy.

One day, some men came to the house.

'Come to Far Far Away!' they said. 'The King and Queen want to see Princess Fiona and her new husband.'

'I don't want to go,' said Shrek. 'They're not going to like me.'

But Fiona wanted to see her mum and dad.

'OK,' said Shrek. 'I'm doing this because I love you.'

'And I'm coming too,' said their friend, Donkey.

After many days, they came to Far Far Away. It was a beautiful place and many fairy tale characters lived there.

The King and Queen and the men and women of Far Far Away waited for Princess Fiona.

'Hello, Mum and Dad!' said Princess Fiona.

'Oh no!' said the King. 'You're ogres!'

CHAPTER 3
The Fairy Godmother's magic

At dinner, the King was angry with Shrek because he and Fiona were ogres. Fiona was very sad. She went to her bedroom and cried.

Suddenly the Fairy Godmother came in.

'It's OK, Fiona,' she said. 'You are going to be beautiful again.'

The Fairy Godmother went to the King.

'Kill Shrek,' she said. 'Prince Charming's going to be Fiona's husband.'

The King went to Puss In Boots.

'Kill Shrek,' he said. 'He's not a good husband for Fiona.'

Next morning, Puss In Boots found Shrek, but Shrek was very strong.

'I'm sorry,' said Puss In Boots. '*The King* wants to kill you, not me!'

Now Shrek, Donkey and Puss In Boots were friends.

The friends went to the Fairy Godmother's magic castle. Puss In Boots found lots of bottles there.

The Fairy Godmother and Prince Charming saw them. They were angry.

'Take a bottle and run!' shouted Shrek.

The friends ran away.

'What are we going to do?' Prince Charming asked.

'I know,' said the Fairy Godmother. 'Listen to me ...'

'What's in the bottle?' asked Donkey.

'*Drink this and be handsome!*' read Puss In Boots.

Shrek and Donkey drank it.

'But it stops at twelve o'clock at night,' said Puss In Boots.

CHAPTER 4
'It's me, Shrek!'

Now Shrek and Donkey were handsome!

'This is great!' said Donkey.

'Fiona's going to be very happy!' thought Shrek.

Donkey found Fiona at the castle. She was beautiful again.

'Wait here for Shrek,' said Donkey. 'He's very handsome now!'

Fiona waited.

'Fiona!' someone shouted. It was Prince Charming.

'Who are you?' she said.

'It's me, Shrek!' said Prince Charming. 'Do you like my new face?'

'I don't know,' she said. 'I liked you before.'

Shrek looked for Fiona. The Fairy Godmother stopped him

'She doesn't want to see you,' she said.

Then Shrek saw Fiona with Prince Charming.

'They're happy,' he thought.

'She's a princess and you're an ogre,' said the Fairy Godmother. 'She can never be happy with you.'

Shrek was sad. Then the King came out of the castle. Shrek went after him.

The King went into a house. Prince Charming and the Fairy Godmother were there.

Shrek listened at the door.

'I'm not Shrek!' laughed Prince Charming. 'But Princess Fiona doesn't know!'

'But she doesn't like you!' said the King.

The Fairy Godmother had a bottle for the King.

'Let's have a party in the castle!' she said. 'Give this magic drink to Fiona before the party.'

'We're going to stop that ogre!' she said to Prince Charming. 'One kiss – and Fiona loves YOU!'

CHAPTER 5
The party

Shrek was very angry.

'I love Fiona!' he said. 'What can we do?'

'I know,' said Puss In Boots. 'The big Gingerbread Man can help us!'

Shrek jumped onto the big Gingerbread Man.

'Now I can go to the party in the castle!' he laughed.

At the party everyone danced. Princess Fiona was not happy, but she danced with Prince Charming. Prince Charming kissed her.

Suddenly Shrek ran into the room.

'Stop!' he shouted.

'Shrek!' said Princess Fiona. 'My husband!'

The Fairy Godmother came into the room.

'She didn't drink from the magic bottle!' she said.

'No, she didn't,' said the King.

The Fairy Godmother was angry. She said something very quickly and very quietly. Suddenly there was no Fairy Godmother and no King!

'Dad!' shouted Princess Fiona. 'Where are you?'

Suddenly she saw a frog. It was the King!

'I'm sorry, Fiona,' said the Frog King. 'Please be happy with Shrek!'

Puss In Boots ran into the room.

'Shrek, it's twelve o'clock!' he shouted.

Suddenly Shrek and Fiona were ogres again, and Donkey was a donkey.

'Now I am happy!' said Fiona, and she kissed Shrek.

And now everyone was happy!

THE END

Real World

IT'S MAGIC!

The Fairy Godmother does a lot of magic in *Shrek 2*. You can learn magic. Some people work as magicians.

The Magic Circle

The Magic Circle is a magic club in London. Some very good magicians are in The Magic Circle. There is also a Young Magicians Club for magicians from ten to eighteen years old. Every year the club has a Young Magician of the Year.

Paul Kieve

Paul Kieve loved doing magic tricks when he was young. When he was seventeen, he was second in the Young Magician of the Year competition.

Now Paul is a magician. He knows a lot about magic. He was Daniel Radcliffe's magic teacher in *Harry Potter and the Prisoner of Azkaban*.

add +

multiply x

subtract −

The 'How old are you?' number trick

Do this trick with a friend!

1. Write your age, e.g. 09 or 10.
2. Multiply the first number by 5.
3. Add 3.
4. Multiply this number by 2.
5. Add the second number of your age to this number.
6. Subtract 6 … and that's your age!

What do these words mean?

people club trick competition age

Do you know any magic tricks? Show them to your friends.

After you read

1 Match the characters and the descriptions.

a) The Fairy Godmother
b) The King
c) Puss In Boots
d) Donkey
e) Princess Fiona
f) Shrek

i) Her mum and dad are King and Queen.
ii) This cat doesn't kill Shrek.
iii) She can do magic.
iv) At the end of the story, he is a frog.
v) He goes to Far Far Away with Fiona and Shrek.
vi) He is a big green ogre.

2 Yes or No? Read and circle.

a)	Does Shrek want to go to Far Far Away?	Yes	No
b)	Does the Fairy Godmother kill the King?	Yes	No
c)	Does Puss In Boots live in Far Far Away?	Yes	No
d)	Does Fiona like Prince Charming?	Yes	No
e)	Does Fiona love Shrek?	Yes	No
f)	Does Shrek go to the party?	Yes	No

Where's the popcorn?

Look in your book.
Can you find it?

Puzzle time!

1 Who is it? Write the name under each picture.

a) the King

b) ....

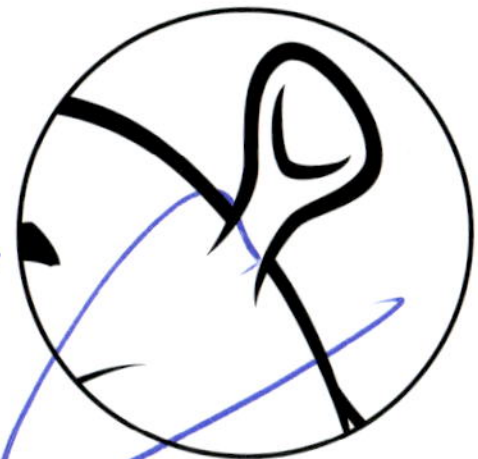

c) ....

d) ....

e) ....

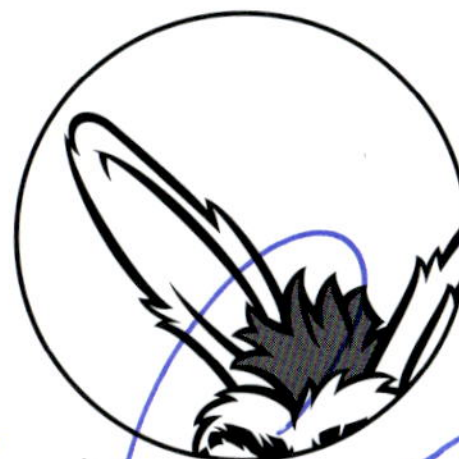

f) ....

2 Which adjectives describe these characters?

angry bad big cool funny
handsome nice old rich strong

big
....
....

....
....
....

....
....
....

3 Complete the crossword.

1		H	U	S	B	A	N	D
2					O			
3					T			
4					T			
5					L			
6					E			

1 Shrek is Fiona's ....

2 The King is now a ....

3 'Let's have a .... !' says the Fairy Godmother.

4 The Fairy Godmother lives in a magic ....

5 '.............................. Shrek!' the Fairy Godmother says to the King.

6 .... is Shrek's very good friend.

4 At the end of the story, the King is a frog. What animal would you like to be? Draw a picture of the animal and complete the sentence.

I would like to be a
....
because ....
....
....
....
....

Imagine ...

1 Choose a well-known fairy tale character. Write three things about him or her.

2 Mime the character to your friends and tell them the three things.

I run very fast. You can eat me. In this story, I'm very big.

You're the Gingerbread Man!

Chant

1 Listen and read.

Fiona's family

There's my dad – the King!
There's my mum – the Queen!
There's my husband – Shrek!
And me – FIONA!

2 Say the chant.

3 Write and say your own family chant.